100 PHOTOGRAPHY PROMPTS

100 Photography Exercises and Ideas to Build Skills and Find Your Artistic Style

For E, L, S, G, O, & A

Third Revised Edition

PUBLISHED INTERNATIONALLY BY TRAVIS FITZGERALD
PHOTOGRAPHY
HTTP://TRAVISFITZGERALD.PHOTOGRAPHY

COPYRIGHT © TRAVIS FITZGERALD LLC 2017-2024

INTRODUCTION	7
THE BASICS	12
1. A PHOTO OF LIGHT	13
2. A PHOTO OF WHITE	14
3. A PHOTO OF BLACK	15
4. A PHOTO OF RED	16
5. A PHOTO OF BLUE	17
6. A PHOTO OF YELLOW	18
7. A PHOTO OF COLOR	19
8. A PHOTO OF LINES	20
9. A PHOTO OF STILLNESS	21
10. A PHOTO OF MOVEMENT	22
11. A PHOTO OF REPETITION	23
12. A PHOTO OF TEXTURE	24
13. DYNAMIC ASSIGNMENT	25
THE WORLD AROUND YOU	26
14. A PHOTO OF WATER	27
15. A PHOTO OF WOOD	28
16. A PHOTO OF THE NATURAL WORLD	29
17. A PHOTO OF METAL	30
18. A PHOTO OF GLASS	31
19. A PHOTO OF STRUCTURE	32
20. A PHOTO OF A DOOR	33
21. A PHOTO OF A WINDOW	34
22. A PHOTO OF INDUSTRY, MACHINERY, OR MECHANICAL	35
23. A PHOTO OF IMMENSITY - OF SIZE ON A LARGE SCALE	36
24. BUILD AND PHOTOGRAPH SOMETHING	37

25. A PHOTO OF CITY	38
26. A PHOTO OF COUNTRY	39
27. TAKE A PHOTO OF A LARGE SCENE, WITH MANY COMPONENTS	40
28. A PHOTO OF LIGHT THROUGHOUT THE DAY	41
29. A PHOTO OF FOOD	42
30. A PHOTO OF VEHICLES	43
31. A PHOTO OF FLIGHT	44
32. A PHOTO OF FAST	45
33. A PHOTO OF SLOW	46
34. A PHOTO OF TRAVEL OR JOURNEY	47
35. A PHOTO OF VACATION	48
36. A PHOTO OF SOMETHING OUT OF PLACE	49
37. A PHOTO OF ANIMALS	50
38. SPONTINAITY	51
39. INTENTIONALITY	52
40. DYNAMIC ASSIGNMENT	53
THE HUMAN ELEMENT	54
41. PHOTOGRAPH SOMEONE YOU KNOW	55
42. PHOTOGRAPH SOMEONE YOU DO NOT KNOW	56
43. A PHOTO OF SOMEONE OLD	57
44. A PHOTO OF SOMEONE YOUNG	58
45. A PHOTO OF YOURSELF	59
46. A PHOTO OF PEOPLE	60
47. A PHOTO OF PEOPLE, WITHOUT ANYONE IN THE SHOT	61
48. A PHOTO OF YOURSELF	62
49. OBSERVING PEOPLE	63
50. THE HUMAN BODY AS LANDSCAPE	64
51. A PHOTO OF DANCING	65
52. A PHOTO OF SOMEONE AT THEIR WORKPLACE	66
53. A PHOTO OF SOMEONE DOING A JOB	67

54. A PHOTO OF SOMEONE DOING SOMETHING THEY LOVE
                                                           68
55. A PHOTO OF SOMEONE DOING SOMETHING THEY HATE
                                                           69
56. DYNAMIC ASSIGNMENT   70
REFLECTION   71
57. A PHOTO OF LOVE   72
58. A PHOTO OF HATE   73
59. A PHOTO OF LIFE   74
60. A PHOTO OF DEATH   75
61. A PHOTO OF HAPPINESS   76
62. PHOTOGRAPH YOUR DREAMS AND ASPIRATIONS   77
63. PHOTOGRAPH DREAMS OF SLEEP   78
64. A PHOTOGRAPH OF SADNESS   79
65. A PHOTO OF SOMETHING THAT SCARES YOU   80
66. A PHOTO OF FAMILY   81
67. A PHOTO OF SOLITUDE   82
68. A PHOTO OF AGING   83
69. A PHOTO OF TIME   84
70. A PHOTO OF PASSION   85
71. A PHOTO OF PEACE   86
72. A PHOTO OF CHAOS   87
73. A PHOTO OF TENSION   88
74. A PHOTO OF SERENITY   89
75. A PHOTO OF SPONTANEITY   90
76. A PHOTO OF DECAY   91
77. A PHOTO OF FEAR   92
78. A PHOTO OF LONELINESS   93
79. A PHOTO OF EXCITEMENT   94
80. A PHOTO OF ENERGY   95
81. A PHOTO OF WHAT OCCUPIES YOUR MIND LATELY   96

82. A PHOTO OF WHAT MAKES YOU HAPPY TODAY	97
83. A PHOTO OF WHAT MAKES YOU SAD TODAY	98
84. A PHOTO OF TERROR	99
85. A PHOTO OF OPPRESSION	100
86. A PHOTO OF FREEDOM	101
87. A PHOTO OF RELAXATION	102
88. A PHOTO OF DISCORD	103
89. A PHOTO OF HARMONY	104
90. A PHOTO OF ISOLATION	105
91. A PHOTO OF CONSTRUCTION	106
92. A PHOTO OF DESTRUCTION	107
93. A PHOTO OF WORDS	108
94. A PHOTO OF MUSIC	109
95. A PHOTO OF SOUND	110
96. A PHOTO OF SILENCE	111
97. A PHOTO OF TRUTH	112
98. A PHOTO OF LIES	113
99. THE MISSED SHOT	114
100. A PHOTO OF POSSIBILITY	115

INTRODUCTION

Photography is both a technical craft and a boundless art form. It's about capturing a moment, a feeling, or a perspective that no one else might see. With countless ways to learn the technicalities—through classes, blogs, videos, or mentors—it's easy to focus on the how and forget the why. This book aims to reconnect you with the why.

"Photography takes an instant out of time, altering life by holding it still."

— Dorothea Lange

Every photo is a unique blend of technical skill and creative expression. To master the former, you need to understand concepts like aperture, shutter speed, framing, and composition. To develop the latter, you need to explore the world through your own lens—literally and figuratively.

Creativity, however, can be elusive. Whether you're a seasoned photographer or just starting, there are moments when inspiration runs dry. You stare at your camera, unsure of what to shoot. This book is here to help you find your way back to your artistic flow.

"You don't take a photograph, you make it."

— Ansel Adams

Each of the 100 prompts in this book is designed to stretch your imagination and challenge your creative instincts. Some are straightforward and literal, while others encourage abstract and emotional interpretations. They are meant to guide, not limit you. Think of them as a spark, waiting for you to kindle a flame of originality.

For example:

"A photo of water" could mean capturing the ripples of a calm pond or the torrential power of a waterfall.

"A photo of love" might be an intimate embrace or a simple flower growing between cracks in the pavement.

"A good photograph is knowing where to stand."

— Ansel Adams

Your journey through this book will be uniquely yours. There are no examples here because this isn't about recreating someone else's vision. It's about exploring what each word or idea means to you—and how you want to tell that story through your lens.

Some prompts will challenge your comfort zone, and that's okay. Push yourself. Venture out of your usual environments. Experiment with light, perspective, and composition. Don't be afraid to fail; every shot teaches you something new.

"To me, photography is an art of observation. It's about finding something interesting in an ordinary place."

— Elliott Erwitt

So, grab your camera—be it a DSLR, a film camera, or just your smartphone—and step into the world with fresh eyes. Whether you're documenting reality or creating fiction, this book will help you uncover your style, hone your craft, and embrace the unpredictable beauty of photography.

"The camera is an instrument that teaches people how to see without a camera."

— Dorothea Lange

Happy shooting!

THE BASICS

1. A PHOTO OF LIGHT

The word "photography" means *light drawing*. Play with light and let it play with the world around you.

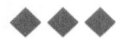

Subject:

Notes on shoot:

2. A PHOTO OF WHITE

Pure, clean, sterile, blinding, or subdued. Religious or medical, blank and boundless. The presence of all light and the absence of all color.

Subject:

Notes on shoot:

3. A PHOTO OF BLACK

Inky darkness, sleek elitism, negative space in form and function, the absence of all light and the presence of all colors.

Subject:

Notes on shoot:

4. A PHOTO OF RED

A primary color; red is the color of love, lust, passion, hunger. It can be found naturally in flora and fauna, or used to express deep, intense, emotions.
Explore yours.

Subject:

Notes on shoot:

5. A PHOTO OF BLUE

Water, sky, pigmentation and cool calmness. Often associated with the concept of the "male"; blue may also represent harmony, serenity, spirituality, confidence, distance, cold, space, and sadness.

Subject:

Notes on shoot:

6. A PHOTO OF YELLOW

Bright and vibrant, subdued and cool. Yellow is the final third of the primary colors to explore.

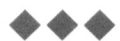

Subject:

Notes on shoot:

7. A PHOTO OF COLOR

Color can add emotion, power, depth, narrative, and form to a photograph. Like the artist with charcoal and pastels, there is a right time and place for each.
Be bold or be subtle - but do it with color.

"Color is a power which directly influences the soul."
— Wassily Kandinsky, *Concerning the Spiritual in Art*

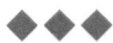

Subject:

Notes on shoot:

8. A PHOTO OF LINES

Leading lines moving your eyes from one space to another, literal lines like railroad tracks to the distance, or suggested lines hinting at form and flow, lines of movement created by the subject, and lines established by the eye as it moves through the final image - explore linear composition.

Subject:

Notes on shoot:

9. A PHOTO OF STILLNESS

Calm, motionless, devoid of movement or placid. Quiet contemplation and motionless passing of time.

Subject:

Notes on shoot:

10. A PHOTO OF MOVEMENT

From a marathon runner streaking across the finish to a piece of paper blowing down the street – even the moment before the movement, the instant of potential energy stored in a batter about to swing. Find energy and capture it in a frame.

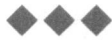

Subject:

Notes on shoot:

11. A PHOTO OF REPETITION

Patterns, actions, form, and function. Look for repetition in its many forms.

Subject:

Notes on shoot:

12. A PHOTO OF TEXTURE

Worn sandpaper, a pile of rugs, the weathered skin on an expressive soul. Something you can feel just by looking at it.

Subject:

Notes on shoot:

13. DYNAMIC ASSIGNMENT

THE SHORT DETOUR

Walk, bike, or take public transit in a random direction for 10-30 minutes. Stop when your timer goes off and look around—what catches your eye first? Now, challenge yourself: can you find something extraordinary in what might seem ordinary? Let curiosity guide you and shoot with intention.

Subject:

Notes on shoot:

THE WORLD AROUND YOU

14. A PHOTO OF WATER

Wet, solid, frozen, gaseous — it can quench your thirst, or drown you. Water covers the globe, adorns our office parks, cleans our bodies, cooks our food, and makes up our bodies. Explore the world of water.

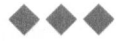

Subject:

Notes on shoot:

15. A PHOTO OF WOOD

From a toothpick to the massive redwoods — we rely on wood to house us, provide furniture for our house, tools, music, entertainment, and so much more. Since the first tools made of stones and sticks, wood has been a part of our interaction with the world.

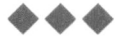

Subject:

Notes on shoot:

16. A PHOTO OF THE NATURAL WORLD

Forests, deserts, mountains, rivers, oceans - living animals flying high and ancient rocks from deep within Earth's inner chambers. A feeling? A physical object? A moment? Rewild. Get natural.

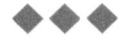

Subject:

Notes on shoot:

17. A PHOTO OF METAL

Metal can be sharp, dull, course, or smooth. It can be hot or cold. Soft, or hard. We use it to build implements of destruction, and sterile tools for medical salvation. We use it to build art to live in and look at or travel; appreciate its many forms and how the light plays across its surface.

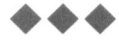

Subject:

Notes on shoot:

18. A PHOTO OF GLASS

Smooth or textured, clear or opaque. From walls, windows, writing surfaces, drinking vessels, to reading glasses and so much more. It is the material through which we look at the small (microscopes), the galactic (telescopes), the outside world (windows), and back at ourselves (mirrors).

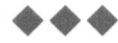

Subject:

Notes on shoot:

19. A PHOTO OF STRUCTURE

Buildings and sculptures, mighty and miniscule – the structures we build to live in, travel across, appreciate as art, and support our world.

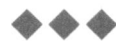

Subject:

Notes on shoot:

20. A PHOTO OF A DOOR

We pass by them and through them every day, the first thing you see when you enter or leave some place. How often do you stop to notice the details? Contemplate the physical appearance and the metaphorical act of 'passing through' as artistic interpretation. Wonder, fear, excitement or trepidation – what is on the side?

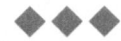

Subject:

Notes on shoot:

21. A PHOTO OF A WINDOW

Looking out or looking in – homes, buildings, cars, trains, planes – we see the world through them, they light our way or let us see where we are not.

Subject:

Notes on shoot:

22. A PHOTO OF INDUSTRY, MACHINERY, OR MECHANICAL

From steam engines to electric cars, planes to submarines, eggbeaters to farm equipment, music boxes and oil drills; mankind has always searched for improved living through mechanization.

Subject:

Notes on shoot:

23. A PHOTO OF IMMENSITY - OF SIZE ON A LARGE SCALE

Sprawling landscapes, endless valleys, towering skyscrapers, cruise ships, and mountain ranges rolling off into the distance. Even the little can be big; the innocuous, magnanimous. Photograph something larger than life or use angles and focus to make your subject massive – regardless of its physical size.

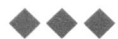

Subject:

Notes on shoot:

24. BUILD AND PHOTOGRAPH SOMETHING

Perhaps a card house, perhaps a real house! A model, a car, a sandcastle, Lego set, cairn or chair – become intimate with the very structure, design, and effort involved in an object – then explore capturing that.

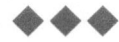

Subject:

Notes on shoot:

25. A PHOTO OF CITY

Metal, brick, glass, and concrete. Life at 100 miles an hour, 24 hours a day, 7 days a week. Remember the cities are more than a place, more than just buildings. They are the architecture, the people, the art, the food, and the humanity within.

Subject:

Notes on shoot:

26. A PHOTO OF COUNTRY

Wide open spaces, rural living, and a slower way of life.

'Nuff said.

Subject:

Notes on shoot:

27. TAKE A PHOTO OF A LARGE SCENE, WITH MANY COMPONENTS

Think and shoot big! A rocky canyon with textures and tones, a cityscape, a marina, a busy street; zoom out and capture it all.

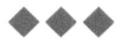

Subject:

Notes on shoot:

28. A PHOTO OF LIGHT THROUGHOUT THE DAY

Pick a window in your home. Set an alert for every hour from sunrise to sunset. Leave your camera in place if possible and try to photograph the scene every hour (or as much as possible) – good or bad. In the moment, and after the final shot; take time to appreciate the changing conditions and the difference in images at different times of the day.

Subject:

Notes on shoot:

29. A PHOTO OF FOOD

Homemade, on the vine, or out of a can. Fresh, rotten, a full meal or a single crumb, cooking, eaten, eating, or presented – fuel for life.

Subject:

Notes on shoot:

30. A PHOTO OF VEHICLES

The things that move our body can also move our emotions, our minds, and state of being. Transportation is often a symbol of freedom, power, or transcendence. It can evoke thoughts of rebellion or conformity.

Find what moves you.

Subject:

Notes on shoot:

31. A PHOTO OF FLIGHT

Natural, organic, artificial, manned, powered, or gliding on gossamer wings – sometimes the action, sometimes the idea.

Always the dream.

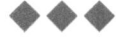

Subject:

Notes on shoot:

32. A PHOTO OF FAST

Speed, motion, and the rush of energy—whether it's a car speeding by, a runner in full stride, or the rehearsed movements of professionals on the job.

Use fast shutter speeds to freeze the action, or slow shutter speeds to capture the blur of movement. Steady your camera to let the motion pass through or track the subject itself.

Fast isn't just about velocity; it's about the feeling of urgency, excitement, or exhilaration. Find it. Frame it.

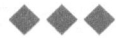

Subject:

Notes on shoot:

33. A PHOTO OF SLOW

The action or the concept, from rusty wheels to the line at your local DMV. Grass growing or the eternity it takes for them to get back to you.

Subject:

Notes on shoot:

34. A PHOTO OF TRAVEL OR JOURNEY

Many of the greatest literary works are built upon tales of adventure, perilous journeys, and life changing experiences on the open road. Consider all the stages of an expedition, the planning, the execution, and the recovery. What takes place before, during, and after?

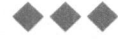

Subject:

Notes on shoot:

35. A PHOTO OF VACATION

Time away, near or far, to step away from the daily grind and escape to a physical place or mental space somewhere else.

We all have a different interpretation of *"getting away from it all."*

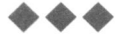

Subject:

Notes on shoot:

36. A PHOTO OF SOMETHING OUT OF PLACE

Find or create something that makes you or someone else take pause and take notice. Humorous, concerning, inquisitive, or elsewhere on the spectrum.

Subject:

Notes on shoot:

37. A PHOTO OF ANIMALS

Timid, loving, terrifying, dangerous; sometimes food - sometimes pets, sometimes threats. Fury, scaley, wet, or flying.

Subject:

Notes on shoot:

38. SPONTINAITY

"To me, photography is the simultaneous recognition, in a fraction of a second, of the significance of an event."
— Henri Cartier-Bresson, The Decisive Moment

Go somewhere outside your living room. Use auto-focus, and shoot from the eye or from the hip, but take what you think is a fine photograph, quickly.

THEN...

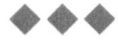

Subject:

Notes on shoot:

39. INTENTIONALITY

Pause, breathe, and take a moment to frame and reframe. Compose with intention.

Take a moment to examine the framing, the use of positive and negative space, the compositional elements, shapes, colors, and pieces of the whole. Reshoot.

Compare the two and assess the difference of the same scene with addition of care and attention. Sometimes taking the extra moment to visualize and craft an image makes all the difference.

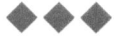

Subject:

Notes on shoot:

40. DYNAMIC ASSIGNMENT

THE MIDWAY ESCAPE

Choose a destination 30 to 45 minutes away by foot, bike, or vehicle—but don't take the most direct route. Meander, follow intriguing side streets, and allow your surroundings to dictate the journey. Along the way, take a series of photos that document the unexpected moments, hidden gems, or fleeting encounters. The journey is the destination.

Subject:

Notes on shoot:

THE HUMAN ELEMENT

41. PHOTOGRAPH SOMEONE YOU KNOW

Direct them for 3 distinct poses/sets. Reflect on the lighting, the mood, and placement. The first one will break the ice, the following two will allow you to engage more intentionally.

Engage, and explore the aspect of direction and communication between artist and subject when there is an established rapport and relationship.

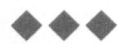

Subject:

Notes on shoot:

42. PHOTOGRAPH SOMEONE YOU DO NOT KNOW

Introduce yourself as a photographer, step outside your comfort zone, explore new dynamics, make new friends, and engaging with a subject you have no established relationship to leverage.

Consider the setting, their individuality, and take their photo. Thank them for their time.

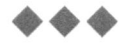

Subject:

Notes on shoot:

43. A PHOTO OF SOMEONE OLD

Mind, body, and/or spirit. Age, experience, and life lived.

What is their story?

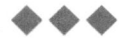

Subject:

Notes on shoot:

44. A PHOTO OF SOMEONE YOUNG

Young at heart, or in age. What will their story be?

If your picture is the first chapter, what will unfold next?

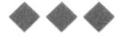

Subject:

Notes on shoot:

45. A PHOTO OF YOURSELF

Include yourself in the frame.

Be creative but include yourself! Go above the selfie and compose something with you in frame; use a tripod and timer or a stack of books, a reflection in a car or window – capture yourself in an interesting way.

Subject:

Notes on shoot:

46. A PHOTO OF PEOPLE

Smiles at a circus or frowns at work, an ocean of concert attendees or a sea of umbrellas from above. Maybe even some strange combination of all of it. Consider repetition, form, and shape.

Capture humans.

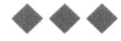

Subject:

Notes on shoot:

47. A PHOTO OF PEOPLE, WITHOUT ANYONE IN THE SHOT

Humans cover the world. Our presence is felt even in the places where we do not live.

Footsteps in the sand and shadows on the wall.

Subject:

Notes on shoot:

48. A PHOTO OF YOURSELF

Without including yourself in the frame!

Different than prompt #45, this captures the 'idea' of you, rather than your physical self.

Consider your hobbies, collections, and the imprint you leave on the world.

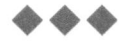

Subject:

Notes on shoot:

49. OBSERVING PEOPLE

Go to a busy place, get a coffee, and observe the space and those around you. Try waiting for at least 30 minutes before taking any photos.

Street and documentary photography takes one deep into the wilderness of the 'human experience'. Become accustomed to being out with your camera, taking in the moment and capturing stories as they unfold.

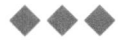

Subject:

Notes on shoot:

50. THE HUMAN BODY AS LANDSCAPE

With its curves and lines, each human figure has a topology as unique as the surface of the Earth. Explore form over function with the human body as a subject of light, form, and storytelling. Consider light, shadow, contrast, and texture.

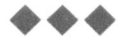

Subject:

Notes on shoot:

51. A PHOTO OF DANCING

Feel the music, the rhythm, and the beat; in form and/or function. Consider the fluidity and motion - the spirit and energy.

Capture the movement.

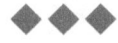

Subject:

Notes on shoot:

52. A PHOTO OF SOMEONE AT THEIR WORKPLACE

Explore using a 'street photography' approach or engage your subject through classic portraiture. Talk to them, ask them how they enjoy their job or what they like about it.
What about their work makes for a captivating image?

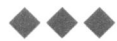

Subject:

Notes on shoot:

53. A PHOTO OF SOMEONE DOING A JOB

Work is not always defined by a 'standard' time and place.

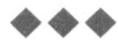

Subject:

Notes on shoot:

54. A PHOTO OF SOMEONE DOING SOMETHING THEY LOVE

Not everything someone does is for a dollar.

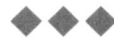

Subject:

Notes on shoot:

55. A PHOTO OF SOMEONE DOING SOMETHING THEY HATE

Through body language or the look on their face — you will know it when you see it.

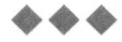

Subject:

Notes on shoot:

56. DYNAMIC ASSIGNMENT

THE FAR FLUNG

Pick a location 45 to 60 minutes away, as far as you can reasonably travel—by car, train, or even hiking. Break out of your usual bubble and head somewhere unfamiliar. While exploring, focus on telling a story: capture the scene as if you were creating a photo essay. Who or what defines this new place? Seek out its essence.

Subject:

Notes on shoot:

REFLECTION

57. A PHOTO OF LOVE

Intimacy, comfort, safety, romance; find it in a look, an action, or subtle moment.

Subject:

Notes on shoot:

58. A PHOTO OF HATE

Subtle or overt; from barbed wire on a compound fence, to a furrowed brow and scowling face. Body language, action, words, and other imagery will help you compose this image.

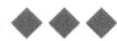

Subject:

Notes on shoot:

59. A PHOTO OF LIFE

Existence, growth, the act of 'being'; the very nature of being alive. Contemplate existentialism and find it through your lens.

Subject:

Notes on shoot:

60. A PHOTO OF DEATH

Enveloping darkness or bright light. Dried flowers, or rotten ones. The end of suffering, or the end of something beautiful. Nothing more, or the start of something new.

Subject:

Notes on shoot:

61. A PHOTO OF HAPPINESS

Subtle pleasure, or raw excitement; smiles and sunshine, mountain tops and rain; happiness can mean different things for different people.

Subject:

Notes on shoot:

62. PHOTOGRAPH YOUR DREAMS AND ASPIRATIONS

What do you aspire to be? What do you aspire to do? Who do you want to be? Where do you want to go?

Subject:

Notes on shoot:

63. PHOTOGRAPH DREAMS OF SLEEP

Emotions of fear or happiness; phantasmal surrealism, or vivid realism. The things we see and experience when we close our eyes can make for cathartic art.

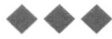

Subject:

Notes on shoot:

64. A PHOTOGRAPH OF SADNESS

Loss, sorrow, discomfort, and displeasure in any outcome. Consider the sadness of yourself and others. Not only as you experience it, but as it is perceived.

Subject:

Notes on shoot:

65. A PHOTO OF SOMETHING THAT SCARES YOU

A shadow, an object, a memory, an idea, or concept – get creative and get scared.

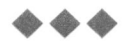

Subject:

Notes on shoot:

66. A PHOTO OF FAMILY

Familial ties can evoke comfort, love, belonging, togetherness, pain, sorrow, guilt, and confusion. Embrace and explore your story or tell the story of someone else.

Art can be an instrument to heal, reflect, and appreciate.

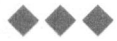

Subject:

Notes on shoot:

67. A PHOTO OF SOLITUDE

Isolation; real or perceived, sought out or received, wanted or unwanted. Find quiet spaces that reflect introspection and peace.

Subject:

Notes on shoot:

68. A PHOTO OF AGING

Time passes quietly, but its effects can be loud.
Change happens subtly or with great impact.

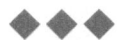

Subject:

Notes on shoot:

69. A PHOTO OF TIME

Time: the mover of mountains and killer of kings.

Explore the idea of time conceptually through content and composition or technically using long exposures, and slow shutter speeds.

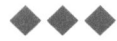

Subject:

Notes on shoot:

70. A PHOTO OF PASSION

The burning fire that fuels love and hate, the words, and actions.

Two sides of the same coin.

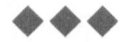

Subject:

Notes on shoot:

71. A PHOTO OF PEACE

An idea, a moment, or relationship between objects or people. Peace can be found on the face of a kind soul on the bus on a benign Tuesday afternoon or between entire armies on a holiday.

Subject:

Notes on shoot:

72. A PHOTO OF CHAOS

Explore anarchy, disorder, and disjointed as visual concepts through compositional elements.

Find - or create - bedlam and capture it.

Subject:

Notes on shoot:

73. A PHOTO OF TENSION

Two people looking at each other expectantly, disaster a moment from occurrence, tightness, and constraint.

Consider including motion or the use of tight framing and cropping.

Subject:

Notes on shoot:

74. A PHOTO OF SERENITY

Calm, quiet, collected.

Breathe deeply and shoot.

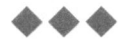

Subject:

Notes on shoot:

75. A PHOTO OF SPONTANEITY

Find or create "lightning in a bottle" and capture it in an image.

GO NOW!

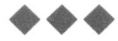

Subject:

Notes on shoot:

76. A PHOTO OF DECAY

As life ends, the corporeal vessel breaks down in a transition to form new life. Seek out the point of transition in the circle of life.

Subject:

Notes on shoot:

77. A PHOTO OF FEAR

Flight or fight...but photograph it either way.

Quickly...before it gets you.

Subject:

Notes on shoot:

78. A PHOTO OF LONELINESS

Solitude without pleasure – a singularity that leaves the subject wanting more.

Subject:

Notes on shoot:

79. A PHOTO OF EXCITEMENT

Standing behind a curtain about to open to a sea of applause; the energy in a leap of faith or opening an acceptance letter from a dream school.

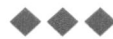

Subject:

Notes on shoot:

80. A PHOTO OF ENERGY

Explosiveness, drive, motion, and the electricity of a moment, an event, or experience.

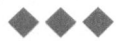

Subject:

Notes on shoot:

81. A PHOTO OF WHAT OCCUPIES YOUR MIND LATELY

More than just work and family; a great many things occupy our thoughts on any given day. An obligation, a success, or failure. Family or friends, a challenge or goal.

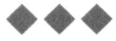

Subject:

Notes on shoot:

82. A PHOTO OF WHAT MAKES YOU HAPPY TODAY

Close your eyes and smile.

What do you think of first?

Subject:

Notes on shoot:

83. A PHOTO OF WHAT MAKES YOU SAD TODAY

Consider the other end of the spectrum. Open your mind to sadness and melancholy. What is the first thing that comes to mind?

Subject:

Notes on shoot:

84. A PHOTO OF TERROR

The kind of fear that takes your breath away and stops you with its icy grip.

Subject:

Notes on shoot:

85. A PHOTO OF OPPRESSION

A flag or a badge, a gun or shackle - the symbols or acts of control.

Subject:

Notes on shoot:

86. A PHOTO OF FREEDOM

Open skies, open roads, broken bonds, and the draw of existence without restraint.

Subject:

Notes on shoot:

87. A PHOTO OF RELAXATION

Little umbrellas in drinks by the ocean, or a hot cup of tea in a mossy cottage. Explore the concepts of comfort, but don't fall asleep in the hammock before you get the shot!

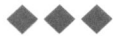

Subject:

Notes on shoot:

88. A PHOTO OF DISCORD

When a point cannot find its counterpoint - the inability for two people, objects, or ideas to find a common ground: dissonance and a lack of harmony.

Subject:

Notes on shoot:

89. A PHOTO OF HARMONY

Everything in synchronicity - form and function, all together. Craft an image expressing this fusion and fluidity.

Consider things like parallelism in lines, balance within composition, and pleasing repetition (both form and concept).

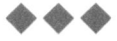

Subject:

Notes on shoot:

90. A PHOTO OF ISOLATION

Alienated, alone, and separated. Explore composition expressing a distance between your subject and all else.

Subject:

Notes on shoot:

91. A PHOTO OF CONSTRUCTION

Bricks, blocks, beams, sticks, and twine. Consider the concept of creation, assembly, and building, both literal and metaphorical.

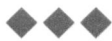

Subject:

Notes on shoot:

92. A PHOTO OF DESTRUCTION

Rubble, broken buildings and broken dreams, scattered remnants of what was – physically, perhaps emotionally.

Subject:

Notes on shoot:

93. A PHOTO OF WORDS

Words can make the image; a tough kid leaning against a wall under a no loitering sign, a person exhaling smoke with a cancer billboard prominently in the background – try to avoid the cliches and find the words that make the photo.

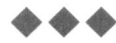

Subject:

Notes on shoot:

94. A PHOTO OF MUSIC

Weathered hands playing an instrument, the swirl of bodies on a dance floor, a stereo by a pool on a sweltering summer day – close your eyes and feel the music envelop you.

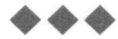

Subject:

Notes on shoot:

95. A PHOTO OF SOUND

Some images are so strong you can feel the elements or hear them through the photograph — a rocket launching, a race car, a screaming baby.

Subject:

Notes on shoot:

96. A PHOTO OF SILENCE

Create an image that pulls you in and creates the feeling of immersion in true soundlessness.

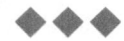

Subject:

Notes on shoot:

97. A PHOTO OF TRUTH

What you see is what you get. Create a photograph expressing the reality of a subject or concept.

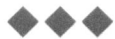

Subject:

Notes on shoot:

98. A PHOTO OF LIES

A contrast to explore how a photograph can manipulate reality, encouraging experimentation with deception in composition.

Subject:

Notes on shoot:

99. THE MISSED SHOT

Find an amazing photo. Nature, people, automotive, city, landscape, sunrise, sunset...whatever...

Visualize it, frame it, but *DO NOT* take it.

The action of taking a picture means you experience life through a lens — take a moment to experience it firsthand, and learn to let the "shot you missed", go.

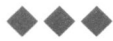

Subject:

100. A PHOTO OF POSSIBILITY

Happy shooting!

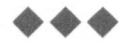

Subject:

Notes on shoot:

www.ingramcontent.com/pod-product-compliance
Lightning Source LLC
Chambersburg PA
CBHW031434210526
45464CB00005B/2197